Getting to Yes

Negotiation Skills & Strategies

By Katie Lenhart
Copyright © 2013

Income Disclaimer

This book contains business strategies, marketing methods and other business advice that, regardless of my own results and experience, may not produce the same results (or any results) for you. I make absolutely no guarantee, expressed or implied, that by following the advice below you will make any money or improve current profits, as there are several factors and variables that come into play regarding any given business.

Primarily, results will depend on the nature of the product or business model, the conditions of the marketplace, the experience of the individual, and situations and elements that are beyond your control.

As with any business endeavor, you assume all risk related to investment and money based on your own discretion and at your own potential expense.

Liability Disclaimer

By reading this book, you assume all risks associated with using the advice given below, with a full understanding that you, solely, are responsible for anything that may occur as a result of putting this information into action in any way, and regardless of your interpretation of the advice.

You further agree that our company cannot be held responsible in any way for the success or failure of your business as a result of the information presented in this book. It is your responsibility to conduct your own due diligence regarding the safe and successful operation of your business if you intend to apply any of our information in any way to your business operations.

Terms of Use

You are given a non-transferable, "personal use" license to this book. You cannot distribute it or share it with other individuals.

Also, there are no resale rights or private label rights granted when purchasing this book. In other words, it's for your own personal use only.

Getting to Yes

Negotiation Skills & Strategies

By Katie Lenhart

Table of Contents

Introduction – What is Negotia-tion?

Interestingly, the world around you is a negotiating table. Whether you like it or not, you will come into conflict with others at some point, and if you're lucky, you end up on the winning side. However, things can turn ugly sometimes where you cannot handle the encounter. In short, you don't get what you want and remain far away from what you expected to get.

If you think about it, you'll probably find a number of good reasons for getting into a negotiation. You secretly want to get amazing discounts at your local store. Your boss is prepared to give you a raise and you want to ask for more benefits and money than what you'll get.

There are numerous other occasions where you think about starting a negotiation and just don't know where to start. Before showing you how you can negotiate effectively, let us discuss what negotiations really are.

Basically, negotiation means that you become a little confrontational and grab the right opportunity. People who are shy, hate negotiating because they are quite happy with all what they get. In simple words, all of us want more money, freedom, justice, status and security and there is no harm in gaining more favors from people who can give you all these things.

If you talk about winners, they seem to be people who are competent for the position and have the ability to negotiate and get what they want. When you think about the practical application of this definition, you'll realize that you can become a winner by negotiating both in your professional and personal life.

What's even more interesting is the fact that not many people consider negotiation to be a helpful tool. You cannot expect things to go your way on every occasion. And, if you don't speak or negotiate, others would never know what you need.

In short, successful negotiations can help you close the deal on your terms and this typically leads to a better and higher outcome. There is no shortage of expert ideas on how you should negotiate and much of this advice is coming up in the next few pages.

Negotiation gurus suggest that you have to be extremely confident with a clear-picture mindset when you step into this game. As with any other task, preparation is essential to win the deal. Preparation becomes more important if you don't want to remain clueless at the time when you get to the table.

Successful negotiation is all about reaching a conclusion that is beneficial for you. You have to proceed with a specific course of action and reach a mutually acceptable agreement. Before you get to the table, here are the key elements you have to work on.

1. Your personal objectives

2. Basis for negotiation

3. Objectives on the other side

If negotiation is your request, you have to do your homework particularly if you are new to this game. No matter how familiar you are with your objectives, work on your negotiation style so that you can avoid the common pitfalls.

Remember, being prepared for the task can help you overcome your fears and you can always stay in control. What is a good way to start negotiating? Continue reading to find out more about how you should present yourself to achieve a desirable outcome.

Get Familiar with the Different Styles of Negotiating

Every person negotiates differently, and you can observe how different styles of negotiating can have an impact on the final outcome. Some people negotiate quickly and think that they have a vision or aspiration. A few say "we are awesome at that" and prove to be quite intimidating. Some negotiators are quiet or passive to be exact, and people of this type can be manipulated easily.

The process of identifying different styles of negotiation is not very difficult, so let's start with this process in this chapter. If you have a good look around you, you'll see that many people are confident and know what they exactly want. Not only do they put forward their opinions, but they are also willing to hear what the other person has to say. If you are confident about your negotiating style, you will not be scared of conflict. Actually, you will be more than happy to put your argument forward, most importantly at the right time.

There are 3Cs when you talk about the different negotiation styles. Your style can either be competitive or collaborative. You can also follow a concession trend during negotiations and here's an image to help you get familiar with the different styles.

Collaborative Negotiation

Also known as constructive negotiation, collaborative negotiation treats the relationship as a very important and valuable element. You can either go with a win-win approach or resort to a joint problem solving approach.
In a collaborative win-win approach, both parties assume that they have gained something valuable at the end. The result however may not be very satisfying even if you emerge successful after the negotiation. Remember, you feel more comfortable when all your needs are met regardless of what the other party gets.
Joint problem solving approach is another thing you can adopt when both parties are willing to

solve a problem. You can act in a collaborative way and take a more objective based decision to get rid of the issue you are facing at that point in time.

Can you face a problem during collaborative negotiation? Well, things may not turn out well when the other person possibly sees your willingness to work together as a weakness. Remember, collaborative approach does not mean that you are weak. Instead it represents that you want to gain the best possible solution where both the parties have something to cheer about at the end.

Competitive Negotiation

As the name suggests, competitive negotiation treats the entire process as a competition where only one person can emerge as a winner. That is, if you gain something, you get what you want. But the other person loses out and does not get a piece of the pie.

You'll find that competitive negotiations are more aggressive and all dealings are done in a hard way. You will only be concerned with what you get and your relationship with the other party is wiped out of the equation completely. Interestingly, if you show any concern for the other person in a competitive negotiation, people may assume that you are either weak or you have plans to deceive them. Typically both the parties don't care about each other in a competitive negotiation and the process can get really heated.

Those who do stick to a competitive approach during negotiation can get assertive and they are often unwilling to cooperate. What's the easiest to find out whether or not the person is competing in a negotiation?

Well, competitive negotiators try to turn the situation in their favor and only focus on their needs. They would also try everything that is possible to win the race rather than sitting down and finding the best solution.

Concession Negotiation

In addition to competitive and collaborative styles of negotiation lies concession, where you do have lots of consideration for others. People who adopt a concession style put themselves at the back and increase the importance of others.

If you follow a concession approach, you can think more about the other person and prioritize their needs. Your own needs will be left behind and there are chances that you end up in a lose-win situation with you on the losing side

Concession negotiation often is interpreted as giving way too much to the other party. People who use this style are afraid of conflict and tend to be submissive. Typically if you don't have any intentions of getting into an argument, you will neglect your own needs.

Is There a Way Between?

Between competitive and collaborative negotiation style there is a narrow path. Here you can apparently act as a competitive negotiator during the deal and become best friends with the other party once negotiation gets over. The key to being successful with the way in between is to adapt your style and find an effective solution.

Summary of Different Negotiation Styles

Competitive Negotiation
• There is no room for relationships

• Consider only yourself

• Focus on your own position and needs

• Aim to gain sole advantage

• The outcome will only be win or lose

Collaborative Negotiation

- Relationships do matter

- Consider a solution that benefits both parties

- Focus on mutual interest

- Aim to close the deal on fair agreement

- Stick to rightful principles

- Win-win situation for both

Have a Look at the Common Personality Types in Every Negotiation

We all have different personalities and there are times when you have problems negotiating with the other person. Knowing the different personalities you can come across during the negotiation process can help you become more comfortable.

There are four different personality styles and each responds to a different negotiating style. They include dominant or driver, communicator or expressive, interactor or amiable and last, perfectionist or analytical.

Drivers or dominant personalities as you would sense are determined people and love to be in control. They can be stubborn, often impatient at times, but there is nothing that shifts their focus away from the task. You may come across "drivers" who are extremely inflexible and may not listen to you.

If you sense that the other person belongs to this category, you have to do your homework right. Plan to ask specific questions and focus more on results. It is better if you use facts to support your discussion because personal experiences are the least effective tool you can use to convince a dominant personality.

On a separate drivers are not really impressed by negotiators who invade their personal space.

The second type of category you would come across is "expressive or communicator." As the name suggests, people who are expressive are more responsive and enthusiastic about the negotiation.

They also have flexible agendas and are willing to listen to what you have to say. Expressive negotiators pay more attention to relationships and have the ability to make creative decisions.

Don't be surprised if the person sitting right in front of you is talkative and looks optimistic. Just remember that expressive negotiators are emotional and you can handle them in a friendly manner.

If there is anything you want them to agree on, simply discuss the issue in a friendly manner and your work will be done.

The third negotiator you would come across is an interactor or amiable personality. Typically, amiable negotiators are not goal oriented and they love to be everybody's friend. They don't take risks and at times, can depend heavily on you (the other party) to reach to a decision.

Working with amiable personalities gets really easy if you find a common ground. You can find more about their personal interests and focus your decision on how you can achieve a successful outcome.

Even though amiable negotiators are not tough to get along, you may have to be patient at times. Often negotiation with an amiable person is not an easy pushover as they can take time to agree on a solution. All you have to do is stick to your plan and give them low risk solutions to get what you want.

Finally you would come across perfectionists or analytical personalities. They want everything to be in writing and in precise order. Perfectionists have amazing control over their behavior and prove to be excellent problem solvers. Although perfectionists have rigid requirements, it is easy to convince them when your discussion is backed by logics and facts.

The easiest way to negotiate with analytical personalities is to take more action and speak less. Don't overstate the details, rather make sure that your decision is based on logic.

You know that negotiation is a communication process to help two individuals or parties reach a compromise. During the process, you have to keep a close eye on your own interest as well as the opposing party. Like any other task, successful negotiation requires planning and preparation.

Before moving ahead, let's first find out what exactly you should try to achieve at the end of the negotiation process. Experts suggest that you enter the negotiation with a collaborative, rather than a competitive approach. Remember, negotiation is not all about achieving "victory". The end result should favor you and it should at least improve your gain.

Another element you have to consider is whether or not you should bring in extra people or team members. Well, this decision needs to be separate for each negotiation and it also depends on the potential advantages you are willing to gain.

You have to remember that bringing in extra people can be harmful especially if they don't know their role. Your overall position can weaken if there is a difference of opinion within the team. If you have to go ahead with a group, make sure every member of your team is aware of their respective roles.

If you want to be a better negotiator, you've got to find the deal that is best for you. You can work together happily with the other party to get what you want. The key to successful negotiation is seeing the entire process as something that can be resolved with a creative solution.

Your main idea should be not to attack the person sitting in front of you, rather get to the core of the issue. The next chapter tells you more about how you should prepare yourself for the process and come out victorious at the end.

How Can You Negotiate Effectively?

Practically every person you interact will tell you a story about their negotiation encounter. Some of them might have faced an opponent who behaved ridiculously while others will you tales where the person sitting in front of them only sat there and didn't even say a word.

Interestingly, it is never easy to predict the kinds of personality you have to deal with during your encounter. Experts suggest that most successful negotiators have one trait in common. They ask relevant and logical questions and at the same time, they are good listeners.

Often you can get what you want by cleverly supporting your arguments. All you have to do is find out what exactly the other person cares about. You will be surprised to know that people often lose their negotiations only because they have a weakness to talk excessively.

Remember, talking less will hurt no one, but talking excessively can push you into an emotional confrontation and you are more likely to screw up the entire conversation. Imagine how frustrated you would feel if the other person is only wasting your time and there are no chances of reaching a mutual agreement.

Some of you would be thinking to go with a competitive approach, but do you think you will be able to handle the heat of a negotiation? Only if you had prepared in advance, you can get what you want without looking like a jerk.

We did discuss this earlier, but let's go over the basics of the negotiation process once again.

1. Negotiation should separate people from the problem. You have to tackle the problem or issue, rather than attacking the person sitting in front.

2. Set your ego aside and focus on what you want to achieve. You can write down a variety of possible solutions before getting to the table. Remember, your vision and creativity can be affected by the pressure involved in the negotiation.

3. Negotiations that consider a beneficial mutual end result work best in most cases. It is better if you ask logical questions in a diplomatic manner to reveal what the other party wants. Your main purpose should be to gain information from the other side.

4. You also need to know how you should handle the situation if the end result is unacceptable to you or the other party.

5. If there is something that can be resolved easily, you must not create panic. Remember, panic can complicate things and it is surely not the way to achieve a successful outcome.

What is the best strategy to achieve your goals? The right thing to do is outline your plan of action and this is exactly what we are going to dis-discuss in the next section.

Step One: Define Your Plan

The first question that would come into your head is "Why Plan?" Interestingly, the stats reveal that people who plan their negotiations have more successful outcomes than those who don't prepare.

So now you know that you need to plan, but what exactly should you "know" before you get to the table.

1. First of all, you have to get familiar with other party's interests.

2. You also need to know the negotiation reputation and style of the other party.

3. Needless to say, you have to pull out information about other negotiations the other party might have had. It is better if you get a clue about the strategies and tactics your opponents use.

4. Experts suggest that you need to have a clear understanding of when your opponent might walk away from the negotiation.

5. Last, you have to know about the resources that are available to the other party.

Once you are done with the first step, get ready to design a negotiation game plan. Here is a figure to help you understand what all you need to consider.

Most successful negotiators identify the "communication" elements they intend to use at this very stage. You can decide:

- The tone you will use for negotiation

- Body language that will complement your negotiation tone

- Data, stats, questions and objective you will put forward

- The strategy you will use to persuade your opponent

As we've seen earlier, negotiation plan is what really makes or breaks your deal. Inadequate preparation or failure to identify the opponent's goals can cost you dearly in the long run. Remember, a well designed negotiation plan not only considers your issues, but you have an understanding of the interest of the other parties involved.

The worst thing you can ever do in a negotiation is failing to know your opponent. While you don't have to be very familiar with the other party, it is definitely not wise to remain seated and do absolutely nothing. What's even fatal is the fact that you assume things in the planning phase. Remember, making assumptions about the other party can hide the core issues and you will be prevented from achieving a successful outcome.

How Can You Research About the Other Party?

Well, there are a number of resources you can use to know more about your opponent. You can use your personal and professional contacts and relationships for information. Moreover, you can always use social media and the internet as a part of your research.

The only thing you need to focus at this point is that your research should be perceived well by others. There are three key factors you must assess, not assume before beginning a negotiation process.

1. Concerns

2. Interests

3. Emotions

Skilled negotiators take out time to identify their own interests as well as figure out what the other party wants. You are more likely to have a collaborative negotiation when your interests are mutual. On the other hand, competitive negotiation becomes an important part of the equation when your interests are contradictory.

Like every other task or job, all parties have "concerns" when it comes to successful negotiations. Failure to identify or address the core concerns right at the start does hinder successful negotiation.

Identifying emotions involved in the negotiation process is an important part of the planning process. Remember if emotions are ignored, your negotiations may not have a successful outcome.

Once you identify your interests and concerns, it is time to prepare and anticipate how your opponent will respond. Brainstorm outcomes that are likely and highlight areas you feel can become a primary source of disagreement. It is a wise move to practice "possible outcomes" so that you get a head start.

Making a Successful Plan

Identifying your goals and interests is the first step in planning the negotiation process. Remember goals and objectives you set have a direct impact on your negotiation strategy.

What's really important to understand at this point is the fact that "wishes" are not goals. There is no limit to what your goals can be, but you need to confirm that your goals and objectives are specific and realistic.

Often your relationships are at stake during negotiations and you have to consider the impact your goals and objectives can have on the future of your relationships.

Once you are done with the goals, you have to move to the next step, which is mapping out a negotiation strategy. The strategy you define basically outlines the way you will work to achieve your goals.

The third important step in making a negotiation plan is understanding the flow of the process. Your negotiation process will have three different phases namely:

1. Beginning or Initiation (this is where you begin your negotiations.)

2. Middle or Problem Solving

3. Ending or Resolution

Before moving to the next section, here's a summary of what we've discussed until now.

- ***Prepare well for the negotiation process.***

✓ Write down your goals

✓ Know what you want and why you want it

✓ Know how you will work with the other party

✓ Write down how you can present your arguments clearly

- ***Understand your relationships***

  ✓ Identify mutual interests and concerns

  ✓ Know how you can achieve an outcome that is beneficial for both of you

- ***Collect information***

  ✓ Learn more about your opponent through your professional and personal contacts.

  ✓ You can also use the internet and social media.

- Know your alternatives

  ✓ How will you react if the other party refutes your argument

- Get familiar with the negotiation protocol

  ✓ When will the process take place

  ✓ Who will be present

  ✓ What will you discuss

Step Two: Express Your View

Often, you'll find yourself negotiating with rude, aggressive or bad-mannered people. In such a situation, negative tactics or aggression from your side will not damage your own reputation, but you may drift away from your goals.

Interestingly, a lot of people get angry or aggressive only to dictate the outcome of a negotiation or intimidate you. At this stage, your only objective should be to remain calm. Remember, you don't have to react or say anything no matter how angry or frustrated you are. Relax and compose yourself and utilize your energy in a positive way.

Even though the statement may sound shocking to some of you, rude and aggressive people are not actually difficult to handle. Sometimes, negotiation can become stressful and people can react in an unacceptable or uncommon manner. Before you get angry and lose your cool, put yourself in the other person's shoes and see if you find a reason for such unacceptable behavior.

You might not be pleased to hear this, but the way you express your views does have an impact on how the person sitting in front of you. This however, is not an excuse to justify rude or aggressive behavior. Remember, the way you communicate can normalize the discussion and you can achieve more successful outcomes.

Ask yourself a simple question. "Is my behavior contributing to the other person's behavior?" However, you have to remember that it's not always your fault that prevents you from achieving your goal. You may be dealing with an angry head who doesn't want to listen to you.

So, you can say that negotiation sometimes is a piece of cake, but it can become tough work. What you need to do is be realistic and understand that negotiations can be difficult. You can resolve even the toughest issues if you are creative and have the ability to present your issues in a convincing style.

When you know about the other person involved in the negotiation process, it becomes a lot easier to express your views effectively. The situation is less likely to become volatile and it's rare that you find yourself walking away from the deal.

Experts suggest that a significant part of your success comes from the way you present yourself during a negotiation. Be positive and concentrate on the three important "Vs" while expressing your views.

1. Verbal – the words you speak.
2. Vocal – the tone you use to convey your statements.

3. Visual – your body language during the conversation.

Studies also reveal that 70% of mistakes are made in the three areas that are highlighted above. If you step into a negotiation with a bad mood, you'll never have a clear mind to explore the options that are available. Moreover, there are chances that you jump to conclusions and mess up the entire thing.

On the other hand, the more you make it seem that things are getting out of hand, the other party would also resist communication and you are destined for a deadlock.

What do you need to do? Honestly, don't expect the person sitting in front of you to read your thoughts. You should share your views clearly and most importantly, don't get mad or express your anger even if the other person is getting aggressive.

Remember, people focus on what you looked like more than what you said. Don't just read out your notes, get the other party involved and be yourself. Find a way to explain your audience what exactly you want to achieve. Start with a friendly tone and avoid presenting too many arguments at the same time.

It is better if you avoid using "negative" or "insulting" remarks to support your claim and make sure you have sufficient logical evidence to back up your negotiation interests.

Here are some useful tips you can use to improve your communication.
1. Avoid sounding "pushy".

2. Focus more on the solution you want to achieve.

3. Take responsibility for your action, don't start a blame game.

4. Look towards the future and forget the past.

5. Say what you want to achieve, not what you hate.

6. Share positive information rather than accusing the other party.

7. Be optimistic and believe that you will be able to achieve a successful outcome.

Remember, there's a good chance that the other party is impressed with your positive attitude and excellent communication skills. And, this can make them more open to persuasion.

Step Three: Listening Does Make Sense

Basically, listening in a negotiation is as important as or even more important than plain talking. Most problems that arise during a negotiation are due to poor listening skills. Experts suggest that it is really worth the effort to pay attention to what the other side is thinking. This is because you can then change your plan and adjust your strategy in the way that'll help you achieve a successful result.

Well, you will also be pleased to know that the best listeners often prove to be the best negotiators. Do you wonder what the reason is for such an amazing track record?

Negotiations often get heated and people end up doing the exact opposite of what they were supposed to do. Think about it, even you feel inclined to do the exact opposite to ideas the other party puts forward.

You already know that you have to gather a lot of good information for a successful negotiation and your ears can help you do just that. You can become a successful negotiator and a good listener by asking relevant questions that reflect your understanding. Before moving forward to the next section, let us first see how you can become a good listener.

- You have to be really motivated to listen to the other party. Remember, the more you hear, then you'll be in a better position to state your facts.

- If you want to ask questions, you must stick to two important goals. First, your questions have to be specific and second, you must try to uncover the other party's needs and wants. Stick to open questions that relate to the topic you want to explore further.

- Your strategy to listen more can really help in the long run as you will be able to pay close attention to the nonverbal clues your opponent gives. Remember, it is equally important to understand the motive behind the gestures, facial expressions and tone the other party uses.

- It's amazing to see how much careful listening can help you during the negotiation process. Try not to interrupt the other person because when you interrupt the other person, you may be cutting off important bits of information that can help you later.

- Giving exclusive attention to the speaker makes the other person feel more valuable. You can occasionally say "yes" or give nonverbal acknowledgements such as a friendly smile or a nod to let the other person know that you are willing to listen.

Active listening does help you negotiate in a better way because it avoids misunderstandings. The other person knows that you want to look at the other side of the picture and this attitude does help people to say more.

The worst thing you can ever do in a negotiation process is not responding to what the other person has said. Putting it simply, if you fail to ask questions or show an inattentive body language, the other person feels that you are least interested in knowing what they are talking about.

Another important thing you need to understand is that it is impossible to speak and listen at the same time. Doing the same can have disastrous outcomes especially when you or your opponent gets into an angry mode.

If you get angry, you might not be willing to hear what your opponent has to say. Moreover, you can jump to a wrong decision which can likely result in you losing control over the negotiation process. Remember, if you have to react to a comment or statement made by the other party, react to the message, not the speaker. Your opponent can walk away from the negotiation if you lose control over your emotions.

Step Four: Handling Deadlocks

Even though the parties involved in the negotiation process have some common interests, you'll come across different objectives and opinions from both the sides that can create a deadlock.

Personally, you don't like it when the other person raises objections or asks you a number of questions. At the beginning, both you and your opponent consider that getting into a negotiation process is the best way to solve your problems. However, during the process, you will be tempted to maintain your stand and push the other party to change.

If you recall the discussion we had earlier, you know that it is essential to outline a few alternatives as a part of the negotiation planning process. You need to figure out what you have to do in case of deadlocks.

Deadlocks during negotiations can arise for a variety of reasons. You are more likely to face a similar situation when both parties have different objectives. Deadlocks also become certain if one party becomes rigid and does not want to keep the negotiations alive.

How can you break these barriers? Well, you need to have a proper plan to handle deadlocks. Here are a few tips that can help you resolve a problematic situation.

- Identify whether your disagreement is good or bad.

- Figure out how much you will suffer if you don't reach an agreement.

- Find out whether this deadlock will cut out better opportunities in the future.

- Identify if there's any other point you can agree on.

Once you figure out the alternatives, develop a list of actions you might take if no agreement is reached. Try to use more promising ideas and convert them into practical options you can use later.

Another thing you need to consider at this point is the fact that positive moods have a positive impact on the negotiation process. If you are in a good mood, you can find a better answer to "what is it going to cost you if you don't reach an agreement?"

A good negotiator always tries to get rid of minor problems in order to avoid a deadlock. Here's some friendly advice to help you avoid your negotiations ending abruptly.

1. Avoid direct confrontation and don't get into arguments.

2. Listen to what the other person has to say.

3. Figure out the reasons for the deadlock and identify possible solutions that can help you get rid of this problem.

4. Take a small break to gather your thoughts and ask effective questions. The language you

use can help you handle your disagreements effectively.

For example, if you don't agree with any point, you could say something like "can you please clarify that" or "I'm afraid this will not work". You don't have to sound confrontational and say that "you are wrong" or "no, that's simply out of question".

Some negotiators simply lose their cool and use statements like "I don't see the point of staying here" or "no, I'm not really interested in talking with you further". Remember when you are dealing with a deadlock or a disagreement, you have to look for solutions. Your ultimate goal should be to find an answer, not complicate the situation further.

Perhaps asking for suggestions and making a few of your own would work best in this case. Use statements like "what would you like to suggest" or "can this problem be solved by..."

Depending on the level of negotiation you have reached, a polite statement during the deadlock could very well be just what's needed. You will be surprised to see the results when you find a solution that works for both sides. But you have to careful. Sometimes you might be giving too much to the other side, which is not really needed. Take your time and come up with a solution that suits your interests and is acceptable to the other party as well. Remember there are solutions that can get things moving again for both of you.

Step Five: Winning At All Costs

Even you wish to win every single negotiation you enter and there's nothing wrong with it. You work hard and plan for the process, so why not you use the opportunity to get some great deals? Interestingly, no one likes to lose in a negotiation, and the best part is now you will never lose, but only if you follow the helpful tips mentioned below.

Firstly, before you start or even get to the table; you have to figure out your best alternative. We did discuss about this during the planning process and your best alternative is known as "BATNA" or the Best Alternative To Negotiated Agreement.

Once you've established your BATNA, you have to identify ways you can control the direction of the negotiation. One of the best ways to ensure that you always win in a negotiation is using the right style at the right time.

You can use a competitive style of negotiation when you require a quick, decisive action on an important issue. This style is also appropriate when you know that you're right and the other party is only looking to gain advantage of your humble attitude.

A collaborative style of negotiation usually works best in cases where you have to find a solution that benefits both the particles. Often negotiations have interests and concerns that are important to both the sides and you simply cannot compromise. Collaborative negotiation makes sure you address the real issues and don't get a push back. Once you've identified the crucial problems, collaborative negotiation also helps you come with a plan that is easy to implement for both the sides.

If you feel that the core issues are getting neglected or you see no chances of a successful outcome, the best thing you can do is avoid further negotiation. Allow other people to cool down and regain an understanding of the negotiation process. Remember, avoiding negotiation for some time will also help you get knots out of the process and achieve a successful outcome.

Even though it sounds shocking, you can also win a negotiation by adopting a compromising style. This approach works best when you are committed to achieving a result that benefits both sides. Compromising negotiation can also be a good backup plan in case collaborative or competitive negotiations are unsuccessful.

Do you wonder if there's a way to get what you've always wanted in a negotiation? Interestingly, it is highly likely to find a person who has everything he or she "wanted". You can create a win-win negotiation and get what you want.

Here are some quick ideas to help you get started.

1. Do your research and planning instead of trying to overcome other people.

2. Make sure you have an agenda and stick to it closely.

3. Don't forget or neglect the needs of the other party throughout the process.

4. If you feel you've reached an agreement, take the time to highlight it.

5. Be strong and have the right attitude.

6. Keep the other party interested in the negotiation, but don't become predictable.

7. Stay friendly and open during the process. You can also use humor to lighten up the negotiation process.

8. If the other party proposes an impossible demand, your silence can be a sign of your strength. It is better if you stay quiet and if you want to ask a question, make sure it is realistic. The person sitting in front of you will soon realize that this demand is unacceptable and that he or she has "crossed the line".

9. Remember that negotiations are an uncertain process, so take of one small step at a time.

10. It is always best to stick to your plan, but you can have some room for flexibility.

11. Get your facts right and be prepared to answer any questions.

12. Don't lose your self-esteem and confidence even if things are not going your way. Just think that maybe it's not the right time.

What Should You Do If

A) The Other Side is Acting Too Smart

There are quite a few challenges to a negotiation process and you need to try your level best to overcome them. Being too rigid or too smart is one of the biggest obstacles to an effective negotiation. You might come across opponents who try to pressurize or intimidate you. People who act smart tend to show that they have no clue about what you are talking about.

Some people would go a step ahead and say a big "no". However, here's something you need to keep in mind. No matter how rigid your opponent is, there is still a chance you hear a "yes" lat-later on.

Handling over smart negotiators is a tough task, but you can always try your luck. Speak softly and pause for a few seconds after they finish talk-ing. Don't lose your cool and consider overcoming emotional challenges first.

Remember, over smart negotiators would press your "Hot Buttons" thinking that you would ex-plode and turn the negotiation in their favor. But you can always have other plans and still come up with a deal in your favor.

Why would the other party act smart? At times, people give mixed signals just to confuse you. Some negotiators try to act smart to make sure you don't understand their negotiation style. Whatever might be the case, preparing for the unexpected situation beforehand can give you an edge.

If someone is acting smart, you can softly say "wait a minute, you said yes, but your attitude is saying no. Which one should I believe?" This way not only can you take the tension out of the situa-tion, but you give a signal that you too, are a smart negotiator!

B) There is a lot of Risk

You are already aware of the fact that negotiations are very uncertain and you need to take risks. But the question is "how much risk should you take?" Often taking risks in a negotiation can be as simple as asking for more than what you can get, but if you have lots of money involved in the process or your reputation is at stake, the risk can get a little bit too much.

When it comes to taking risks in negotiations, the real question you need to answer is "how much risk is justifiable in your case?" In simple words, you have to select a negotiation and assess the viability of your risk. Here are a few questions that can help you do this.

1. How much risk are you comfortable taking?

2. If you take the risk and the negotiation process doesn't work out the way you had thought at the start, what alternatives or options do you have?

3. What should you do if your plan B does not give the desired results?

The key thing to remember here is that all successful negotiators are willing to take reasonable risks based on logical factors.

C) You Cannot Handle the Pressure

Another negotiation barrier you have to pay attention to is your tolerance level. We all have a threshold at which we are happy, sad or angry and the other person that you are negotiating with will also have the same limits.

If you talk about the most valuable quality of any skilled negotiator, you would know that it is extremely important to remain resilient, particularly under pressure. Your opponent will try every trick in their book to achieve one goal – to sway the negotiation in their favor.

If you want to join the league of skilled negotiators, you have to stand firm no matter how tough the negotiation seems to be. Your resilience and firm stand will eventually help you overcome all the barriers and you will move a step closer towards a successful outcome.

You will be surprised to know that successful negotiators never attach themselves to a specific outcome. This is because if you become "too attached" to the outcome you want to achieve, you will be emotionally involved in the process, which can cause you to make hurried decisions.

Putting it simply, you have to remain in full control of your emotions at all times during the negotiation process.

Remember, one emotional slip will cause you to succumb to pressure and ultimately detach yourself from the negotiation process.

D) You Have to Walk Away From the Deal

Surprisingly, one key factor that really strengthens your position in a negotiation is the ability to walk away from the deal. After reading through the first few pages, you know that negotiation involves finding creative solutions to problems. You have to present your arguments and listen to what the other side has to say.

A lot of negotiations also focus on coming up with a solution that suits both the parties. However, not all negotiations go as planned. You might feel that things are not working out, but do you know when and how you should walk away from the deal?

One of the biggest mistake negotiators make is leaving the table abruptly. The walk away alternative without a doubt can be used as one of the most powerful tools to sideline your opponent, but you have to use it carefully.

You can think about walking away from the deal if:

1. You already have an alternative or back-up plan that doesn't require the other party.

2. Your "Plan B" or alternative plan meets your goals and objectives better than the solution that is proposed on the table.

3. Your opponent uses tactics that are corrupt, unfair or rude.

You can try to reach an agreement through a collaborative approach before you finally step out of the negotiation process.

E) There is no Discussion on the "Issue"

An "issue" is where you make an offer to the other party and if there is no discussion on the issue, there's no point in dragging the negotiation process. If you are well prepared, you will not have problems in going ahead with the deal and being able to reach your target. However, your opponent at times can try to shift your focus away from the core discussion when they sense defeat. What you need to understand is that the lack of clear objectives can never give you a successful result.

You can try to convince your opponent and bring them back to your main area of discussion. Be clear about your objectives and tell them what they will achieve at the end of the process. If things work out, it will benefit both sides, but if your opponent is not willing to cooperate, you can think about leaving the deal.

So, if you find yourself stuck in a situation where the other party is not willing to get involved, spend some time brainstorming about the scenario. Make sure you examine and implement all possible solutions that can help you reach a successful outcome.

You can try your best to stand up to pressure, but don't let others assume your collaborative approach as a weakness. You need to end the negotiation at the right time – something that is more advantageous to you.

Want to Know the Secrets of a Master Negotiator?

Do you know the traits of a master negotiator? Well, following are some key qualities found in master negotiators, and that you should develop if you really want to join the same club.

1. Master negotiators are excellent problem solvers and know the right time to capture an opportunity.

2. To be an expert in negotiations, you need to possess the skills to come up with a creative solution every time you get to the table.

3. Not only are master negotiators well prepared for the process, but they also know what they are going to say, how they are going to present their message and the best strategy that will give them the desired results.

4. Confidence of course, is another key master negotiators possess to gain advantage in any situation. Remember, acting confident will not only help you convince the other side, but they will treat you well.

5. As mentioned earlier, master negotiators have a strong control over their emotions and they are not intimidated by rude responses from the opposite side.

6. In addition, master negotiators are also flexible and can very well change their tactics

during the negotiation process. This especially applies to situations where you end up in a deadlock or there is a possibility of a party walking away.

7. All master negotiators believe in the statement "practice makes perfect". It is always good to play a "negotiation game" before the process actually takes place.

8. When negotiating, master negotiators focus more on what the other party says and take notes. You will be amazed to see the end result when you make the other person feel your commitment.

9. Studies also reveal that master negotiators rely more on facts and ask open ended questions to obtain answers. If you don't understand something that is being said during the negotiation process, you can always ask for clarification.

10. Last, master negotiators can put themselves in the other person's shoes and see what they would do in a situation like this. Remember, a similar approach can help you come up with the best way to resolve a situation so that both parties can walk away satisfied with the end result.

Things You Should Avoid While Negotiating

Even if you are new to the negotiation game, here are some worst possible things you should avoid at all costs.

1. Focusing more on the wrong points or less important issues.

In the previous section, we did mention that there's no point in dragging the negotiation process if you are not talking on the core issue. A common mistake most negotiators do is to get excited about the wrong or less important points. Remember, if you waste your energy on irrelevant issues, you can weaken your position and ultimately get eliminated from the picture.

2. Trying to win every argument.

The most fatal mistake you can ever make is trying to reach a deal which only favors you. Fighting for every argument will only make you look rude and aggressive and the other side will feel that you are being unfair. This might raise questions about your credibility and the other side can simply walk away. Make sure your arguments are fair and reasonable and most importantly are perceived well by others.

3. Making assumptions about the other party.

Most master negotiators spend lots of time researching about the other party and you should do the same. The problem with assuming things is that you will not have a clue about what to do if you encounter an unexpected situation. Remember, it is always better to do your homework instead of panicking at the last minute.

4. Thinking that you are the ultimate decision maker.

This should be a wake up call for those of you who feel that only you can dictate terms during a negotiation process. You know that a number of other people are also involved in the process and you simply cannot make a decision on your own. If you don't want to end up on the losing side, make sure you come up with a decision that benefits all the members involved in the process.

5. Take everything personally.

The most successful negotiators never take anything personally and they are quite open to positive criticism. Whenever you negotiate, remember that is always valuable to stay calm and composed and never show that your opponent's tactic has upset you. Make sure that you grab the emotional advantage during the negotiation process, even if the other party becomes angry or peeved.

The Perfect Ending

At the end of this book, you now know the best way to enter into a negotiation process and how to get the best deal. Remember, your negotiation style may just make the difference in getting what you want or losing the deal. Hopefully you can now deal with negotiations in a way that benefits you, so that a number of good things come your way. It has been a great journey so far and here's hoping that you've enjoyed reading the book. We will surely meet again real soon and until then, the best of luck for an important part of your life that is known as negotiations. Thank you for reading!

www.ingramcontent.com/pod-product-compliance
Lightning Source LLC
Chambersburg PA
CBHW051241170526
45165CB00004B/1520